Dedication

To Amélie Anela Rodrigues -
With much aloha,
Aunty Yuko

Published and distributed by

175 Kahelu Avenue, Unit #4
Mililani, Hawai'i 96789
Orders: (800) 468-2800
Information: (808) 564-8800
Fax: (808) 564-8877
welcometotheislands.com

ISBN: 1-61710-374-8, EAN: 978-1-61710-374-2
First Edition, Fourth Printing—2023
AFO 230702

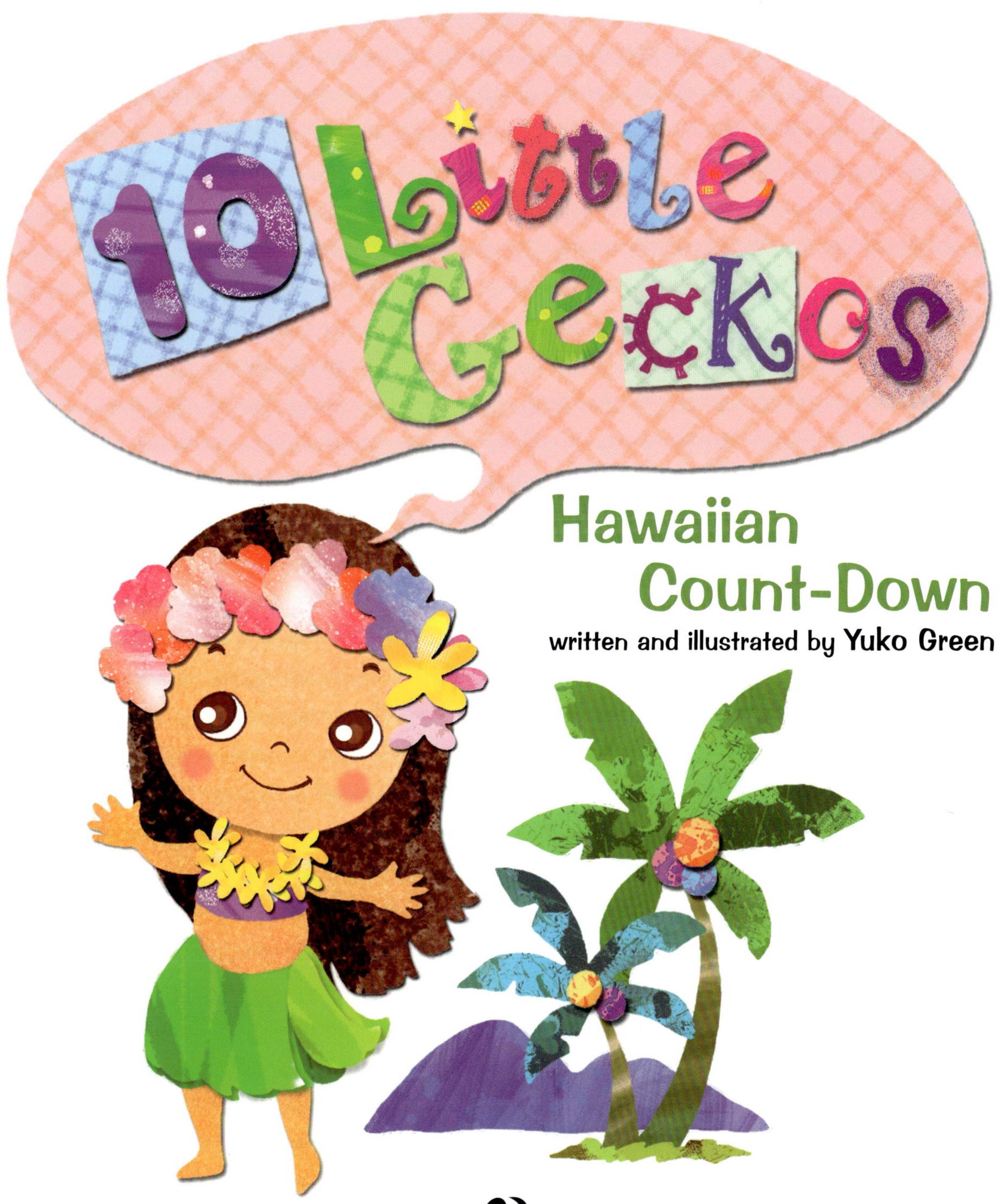

10 Little Geckos

Hawaiian Count-Down

written and illustrated by **Yuko Green**

ISLAND HERITAGE®

Ten little geckos march in a line.

One walks away. Now there are...

Nine little geckos chat by the gate.

One hops away. Now there are...

Eight little geckos sing to heaven.

One dances away. Now there are...

Seven little geckos do some tricks.

One walks away. Now there are...

Six little geckos jump to dive.

One swims away. Now there are...

Five little geckos play on the shore.

One runs away. Now there are...

Four little geckos climb a tree.

One jumps away. Now there are...

Three little geckos play peek-a-boo.

One hides away. Now there are...

Two little geckos lay in the sun.

One rolls away. Now there is...

One little gecko misses his friends.

He goes back home...

And again there are Ten!

The End

1
one
('ekahi)
2
two
('elua)
3
three
('ekolu)
4
four
('ehā)
5
five
('elima)
6
six
('eono)
7
seven
('ehiku)
8
eight
('ewalu)
9
nine
('eiwa)
10
ten
('umi)